FIREPROOF
YOUR MARRIAGE

PARTICIPANT'S GUIDE

OUTREACH®

Fireproof Your Marriage Participant's Guide
Copyright © 2008 by Outreach Publishing

Outreach, Inc., Vista, CA 92081
www.outreach.com

Fireproof Your Marriage is based on the movie FIREPROOF © 2008 by Sony Pictures Home Entertainment and contains concepts and text from Bible studies written by Michael Catt and Stephen Kendrick.

Unless otherwise indicated, all Scripture quotations in this publication are taken from The Holy Bible, New International Version® (NIV)® . Copyright © 1973, 1978, 1984 by International Bible Society. Used by permission of Zondervan. All rights reserved.

ISBN 10: 0-978-71539-X
ISBN 13: 978-0-978-71539-7

Author: Jennifer Dion
Cover and Interior Design: Alex Rozga
Printed in the United States of America

Introduction

In the movie FIREPROOF, Capt. Caleb Holt lives by the old firefighter's adage: "Never leave your partner behind." Inside burning buildings, it's his natural instinct; but in the cooling embers of his marriage, it's another story. For Caleb and his wife Catherine, regular arguments over jobs, finances and bad habits have brought them to the point of saying, "It's just not working out anymore." As the couple prepares to enter divorce proceedings, Caleb's dad asks his son to try an experiment—*The Love Dare*. But can Caleb really love his wife while avoiding God's love for him?

"Never leave your partner behind."

– CALEB HOLT
IN *FIREPROOF*

This six-week small group study is based on the movie *Fireproof,* and it includes video clips from the film as part of each session. We hope you'll relate and be inspired by Caleb and Catherine as they work through all-too-common struggles on their way to an enduring marriage based on God's great love.

In *Fireproof Your Marriage,* you'll be issued a challenge, too—to love first, to love better and to love for a lifetime. Come take the dare!

HOW TO USE THIS GUIDE

The *Fireproof Your Marriage* study is organized into sections:

 FIREPROOF VIDEO

The *Fireproof Your Marriage* DVD has clips from the movie *Fireproof* for each of the six sessions. Each session video is two to five minutes in length.

DISCUSSION

This will be the main portion of the group meeting each week. The first part of the discussion is based on the *Fireproof* session video. The second part of the discussion includes Scriptures that teach on a subject related to the video clip.

FIREPROOF ILLUSTRATION

Each session includes interesting statistics, a Bible story, research or a real-life story as an illustration of that week's teaching. You can either read the illustration aloud during your group, or read the section on your own, before attending your group meeting. The *Fireproof Illustration* provides real-life application and examples that will help you understand and apply each lesson.

FIREPROOFING APPLICATION

Each week, use the *Fireproofing Application* section:

- For personal growth
- As a time of sharing with your partner, to build and strengthen your marriage

The *Fireproofing Application* is divided into three sections:

1. **Fireproofing for Women**
2. **Fireproofing for Men**
3 **Fireproofing for Couples**

Use the *Fireproofing for Women/Men* section for your personal reflection and growth. Use the *Fireproofing for Couples* section to communicate and share with your spouse privately; set aside time together each week to pray and discuss the questions.

> **TIP:** If you're going through *Fireproof Your Marriage* in a small group setting, read your *Fireproofing Application* section as soon as possible after you've met with your group. Reading this section early in the week will give you plenty of time to begin using the verse(s) and respond to the weekly challenge.

As you go through the *Fireproofing Application*:

- Honestly consider your own actions and words—how can you take responsibility for your role in "fireproofing" your marriage?
- Openly share your feelings and needs with your partner.
- Choose your words carefully with a desire to love, respect and encourage your spouse.

These application sections will reinforce the week's teaching and can be a powerful tool for revealing truth and opening up communication.

WEEKLY SCHEDULE FOR SMALL GROUPS

If you choose to study *Fireproof Your Marriage* with a small group, you will meet with your group once each week, and then complete the *Fireproofing Application* section at home. The *Fireproofing for Men/Women* section should take about 30 minutes, and the *Fireproofing for Couples* should take another 30 to 45 minutes.

You might consider setting up a "Date Night" and including the couple's discussion as part of the date.

GUIDELINES FOR SMALL GROUPS

Small groups can have an enormous impact as you build friendships, gain support and encouragement and have a close group of people hold you accountable as you work on your marriage. The guidelines below will help you and your other group members benefit from your time together.

Confidentiality: Remember that everything shared in your small group is to be considered confidential. This protects your group as a supportive, accepting place for its members. Unless you've been given permission, do not share anything from your discussion outside your small group.

Openness: Do your best to be open and honest during discussions. Your transparency will encourage others to do the same.

Respect for Group Members: Remember that each person has the right to their own opinion. All questions are encouraged and respected. Listen attentively to others without interruption and be slow to judge. Be careful about sentences that start with, "You should..." or, "You ought...", and do not give advice that isn't specifically solicited.

Respect Your Spouse's Privacy: During your group discussions, be careful to guard your mate's privacy and feelings. Use the discussions to work on yourself and your relationship with God. If a sensitive issue involves your spouse, and discussing it would embarrass or devalue them in the eyes of the group, save that discussion for the *Fireproofing for Couples* time later in the week.

Priority: Prioritize the small group meeting in your schedule. If you're unable to attend or are running late, call your group leader.

Preparedness: Prepare for the lesson each week and come ready to share.

Participation: Participate in the discussion, but keep your answers brief enough that others can share as well.

Honesty: At any time, feel free to offer suggestions to the leader to improve the study.

Support: Actively support the mission and values of the study and follow the directions given by your leader. Refrain from gossip and criticism; if you have concerns or questions about a member's views or statements, communicate directly with that person.

"So God created man in his own image,
in the image of God he created him;
male and female he created them."

– GENESIS 1:27

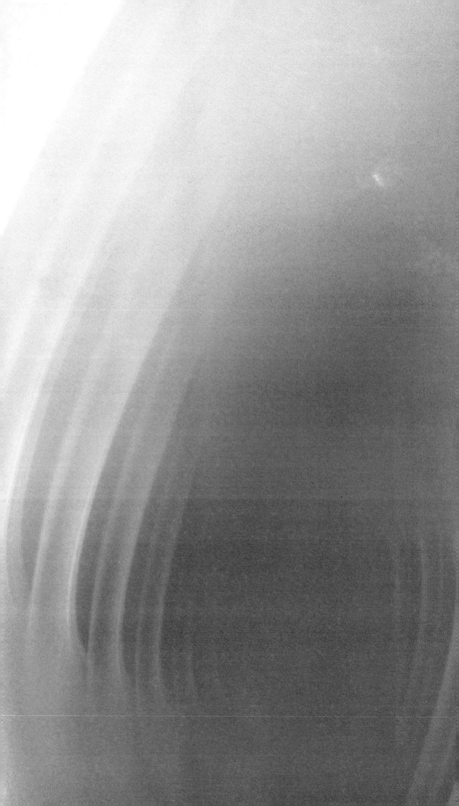

SESSION 1:
He Said/She Said

Open in prayer.

 THE BURNING QUESTION

How do we fulfill our God-given roles in marriage?

 Fireproof Rule of Engagement: Remember that the objective for these sessions is to strengthen your marriage and encourage your partner. If you are doing this study in a small group, answer the discussion questions honestly but be careful to guard your partner's feelings; do not share anything that might embarrass or offend them. Save private thoughts and feelings for the *Fireproofing for Couples* talks with your spouse. Your consideration will encourage a safe environment for discussion and growth.

WARM-UP

Use this section if you're doing *Fireproof Your Marriage* in a small group setting.

ICEBREAKER QUESTION: How did you meet your spouse, and what first attracted you to him/her?

Share your answer with the group.

> "Sometimes I wonder if men and women really suit each other. Perhaps they should live next door and just visit now and then."
>
> – KATHARINE HEPBURN

FIREPROOF VIDEO

Watch the **SESSION 1** video clip on your *Fireproof Your Marriage* DVD.

DISCUSSION

QUESTION 1: Caleb claims Catherine "doesn't _____ him." What word does he use? What emotion(s) do you think he's feeling at the time?

_____

_____

_____

_____

_____

QUESTION 2: Catherine has some complaints about Caleb. What are some of the things she says he doesn't do? Why do you think those things are important to her?

_____

_____

_____

_____

_____

QUESTION 3: Caleb suspects his wife is meeting with her friends and "making me sound like a criminal." How does he seem to feel about Catherine complaining to others about him?

_____

_____

_____

_____

_____

FIREPROOF ILLUSTRATION

 Read the following section either quietly to yourself as you prepare for your weekly session or aloud during the discussion time with your small group or spouse. The *Fireproof Illustration* for each session will include a real-life application or example that will help you understand and apply each lesson.

Jokes about the differences between men and women are timeless and nearly infinite in number. They're told at parties, shared over coffee, and read and forwarded as emails to friends and co-workers. Consider the joke below.

Men are just happier people because...
- *Your last name stays put*
- *The garage is all yours*
- *Car mechanics tell you the truth*
- *Wedding dress: $5,000 Tux rental: $100*
- *Phone conversations are over in 30 seconds flat*
- *Three pairs of shoes are more than enough*
- *You can "do" your nails with a pocket knife*

We laugh over the jokes and teasing stories, but how true are they? Are men and women really that different? One online survey asked people what they thought of the differences. See how you would answer the actual survey question below:

"There is no unisex brain. Girls arrive already wired as girls, and boys arrive already wired as boys. Their brains are different by the time they're born"

– DR. LOUANN BRIZENDINE, UCSF MEDICAL SCHOOL [1]

Indicate your level of agreement with this statement: "Men and women are SO different."
❑ *Yes, worlds apart!*
❑ *Not really, it's all hype*
❑ *I'm never sure*

In the actual poll results, seventy percent picked, "Yes, worlds apart". Eighteen percent chose, "Not really, it's all hype" and twelve percent selected, "I'm never sure".[2]

---

[1] Walt and Barb Larrimore, *His Brain, Her Brain* (Grand Rapids, MI: Zondervan, 2008), 30.
[2] Ibid, 29.

DISCUSSION

 In your group or with your spouse, read Genesis 1:27 and Genesis 5:2.

QUESTION 4: These verses indicate that God deliberately made the two sexes different. Why do you think He chose to do that?

_____

_____

_____

_____

_____

QUESTION 5: If you're studying _Fireproof Your Marriage_ in a small group setting, have the men in your group share one thing they particularly like about women. Have the women share one thing they like about men. If you're studying _Fireproof Your Marriage_ as a couple, share with your spouse what you like about the opposite sex.

_____

_____

_____

_____

_____

Read Ephesians 5:21-33.

QUESTION 6: In this passage, verse 25 gives instructions to husbands, and verse 33 gives instructions to wives. What one word characterizes how a husband should treat a wife? What one word describes how a wife should treat a husband?

_____

_____

_____

_____

QUESTION 7: The passage affirms that God created us male and female—two different creations. As our Creator, He clearly understands how the sexes are different and what our needs are. How closely do you feel God's commands match up with the needs of men and women? Explain your answer.

_____

_____

_____

_____

_____

Read Psalm 139:13-16.

QUESTION 8: What does this passage say about God's knowledge of us?

_____

_____

_____

_____

One survey asked men, given the choice, how they would prefer to feel: "alone and unloved" or "inadequate and disrespected." The survey results are shown below.

Alone & Unloved	76%	
Inadequate & Disrespected	24%	

In addition, the key complaint made by respondents was that the choices weren't different—the men felt being disrespected was the same as being unloved!

QUESTION 9: Do you agree with the results of the survey? Are you surprised? Why or why not?

_____

_____

_____

_____

HOT QUESTIONS FOR MEN & WOMEN

Read and answer the questions in the section below that applies to you. When everyone is finished, share your answers.

QUESTIONS FOR WOMEN

A: Read through the quotes below. Put a check beside the ones that would make you feel most loved, if said by your husband. Why?

❑ *"It sounds like you had a stressful day today. Would you like to talk about it? What happened?"*

❑ *"I really like that new haircut. It makes you look very pretty."*

❑ *(In response to you calling him at work, sounding very upset and asking to talk with him.) "I have some people in my office, but I want to hear what's wrong. Hold on just a minute, and I'll get to a place we can talk privately."*

❑ *"Those boxes are really heavy. Here, let me get them for you."*

B: Read through the quotes below. This time, check the ones that would make you feel most unloved. Why?

❑ *"I know your birthday is tomorrow, but I've been really busy. Here, you can take the credit card and spend 50 bucks on yourself."*

❑ *"I heard John's wife went to that new fitness class and lost 10 pounds. Why don't you go check it out—it might make you feel better about yourself."*

❑ *"When are you going to clean up this house? It's a mess."*

❑ *"Can't you see I'm in the middle of watching the game? You're always wanting to talk about something when I'm trying to relax."*

QUESTIONS FOR MEN

A: Read through the quotes below. Put a check beside the ones that would make you feel most respected, if said by your wife. Why?

❑ "The garage door opener doesn't seem to be working correctly and I know you're better at understanding mechanical things. Would you take a look at it?"

❑ "My husband took the kids out to the park yesterday to give me a break. He's really great about getting me the breaks I need."

❑ "That's great that you got a raise at work. You've earned it."

❑ "I'm having a hard time with my co-worker—he has been undermining me with my boss. What do you think I should do?"

B: Read through the quotes below. This time, check the ones that would make you feel most disrespected. Why?

❑ "You're not really a fix-it kind of guy—don't you think you should call someone to repair that?"

❑ "When are you going to start being responsible and quit spending so much time on that dream of starting your own business?"

❑ "Last night, it took my husband three hours to figure out how to get the new computer working. Technical things are not really his strength."

❑ "When are you going to start making more money at work? We really need to have more income to get all these bills paid."

DISCUSSION

QUESTION 10: Men—share some general comments about what "respect" looks like. Why is respect such a critical issue?

_____

_____

_____

_____

_____

QUESTION 11: Women—share some general comments about how they feel love. Why is emotional connection and understanding so important?

_____

_____

_____

_____

_____

Read Proverbs 15:1 and Ephesians 4:29.

QUESTION 12: What do these passages teach about the importance of communication and using our words to "build up" our spouse?

_____

_____

_____

_____

_____

Close in prayer.

FIREPROOFING APPLICATION

 Fireproof Rule of Engagement: As we struggle in the marriage relationship, we may find ourselves blaming one another for our negative experience. As you share together, remember that the behavior you can most effectively change is your own. Jesus said, *"Why do you look at the speck of sawdust in your brother's eye and pay no attention to the plank in your own eye? How can you say to your brother, 'Brother, let me take the speck out of your eye,' when you yourself fail to see the plank in your own eye?"* – LUKE 6:41-42

Resist the urge to point fingers at one another. Focus on finding and correcting your own flaws so you can personally become more like Christ; this will diffuse anger and ease conflict.

FIREPROOFING FOR WOMEN

Read 1 Peter 3:1-9.

QUESTION 1: Consider Caleb's comments about Catherine's lack of respect. Do you see any similarities in your marriage? Explain.

_____

_____

_____

_____

QUESTION 2: Consider your spouse's answers to the questions about how he experiences respect. What did you learn about his feelings and needs?

_____

_____

_____

_____

Read Ephesians 4:2-9.

On the scale below mark how frequently you use words that "build up" or support your spouse.

├───┤

Very Infrequently   **Neutral**   **Frequently**   **Very Infrequently**   **Frequently**

QUESTION 3: What specific ways will you limit "unwholesome talk" and instead "build up" your spouse? Commit to taking those steps this week.

_____

_____

_____

_____

_____

FIREPROOFING CHALLENGE FOR THE WEEK
Focus on one way in which your spouse feels respected. Commit to implementing it this week in a practical way.

FIREPROOFING FOR MEN

Read 1 Peter 3:7-9.

QUESTION 1: Think about some of the issues Catherine had with her husband Caleb. Do you see any similarities in your marriage? Explain.

_____

_____

_____

_____

QUESTION 2: Consider your spouse's answers to the questions about feeling loved. What did you learn about her feelings and needs?

_____

_____

_____

Read James 1:19.

On a scale of 1 to 5 (with 1 being low and 5 being high) mark how well and how often you feel you listen to your spouse.

1   **2**   **3**   **4**   **5**

QUESTION 3: What are some specific ways you can become a better listener? Commit to taking those steps this week.

_____

_____

_____

_____

_____

FIREPROOFING CHALLENGE FOR THE WEEK
Focus on one way in which your spouse feels loved. Commit to implementing it this week in a practical way.

 FIREPROOFING FOR COUPLES

Open your time together with prayer, asking God to give you wisdom as well as a receptive heart and mind.

 Read Ephesians 5:21-33.

QUESTION 1: Take turns sharing your thoughts about this passage. What phrases or ideas stood out to you? Explain.

_____

_____

_____

_____

_____

QUESTION 2: Share your answers to the men's and women's sections on respect and love. Do any of your spouse's answers surprise you? Ask questions; clarify anything your partner finds confusing.

_____

_____

_____

_____

_____

QUESTION 3: Men—share a few ways in which your partner can best show you respect.

_____

_____

_____

_____

_____

QUESTION 4: Women—share a few ways in which your partner can best show you love and understanding.

_____

_____

_____

_____

_____

QUESTION 5: Take turns sharing a trait you especially appreciate in one another.

_____

_____

_____

_____

_____

Close in prayer.

"We love because he first loved us."

– 1 JOHN 4:19

SESSION 2:
He First Loved Us

Open in prayer.

 THE BURNING QUESTION

Do you know God's love?
Do you reflect that love to your spouse?

 FIREPROOF VIDEO

Watch the **SESSION 2** video clip on your *Fireproof Your Marriage* DVD.

 DISCUSSION

QUESTION 1: As the conversation begins, Caleb talks to his father about his relationship with Catherine and how she is responding to *The Love Dare*. What emotions show in his face and his words? Discuss in your group why Caleb might feel the way he does.

_____

_____

_____

_____

_____

QUESTION 2: Think of a time when you tried to show love to someone, and they didn't respond in the way you wanted. How did you feel? In what ways do you empathize with Caleb in this scene?

_____

_____

_____

_____

_____

_____

"How am I supposed to show love to someone who constantly rejects me?"
– CALEB HOLT

"You can't love her, because you can't give her what you don't have."
– JOHN HOLT

QUESTION 3: Who do you think is more important to Caleb, himself or his wife? What does he say that leads you to your conclusion?

_____

_____

_____

_____

_____

QUESTION 4: When Caleb asks his father, "How am I supposed to show love to someone who constantly rejects me?" his father re-directs Caleb's eyes to the cross. What is John Holt implying? How does the point apply to Caleb?

_____

_____

_____

_____

_____

FIREPROOF ILLUSTRATION

Read the following section either quietly to yourself as you prepare for your weekly session or aloud during the discussion time with your small group or spouse.

AN IMPOSSIBLE LOVE

It was a scene straight out of a romantic movie. A young, beautiful Mexican-American dancer lifted herself from a hotel pool, her exotic features and fit body catching the eye of Michael Franzese, a powerful 32-year-old businessman sitting poolside. Years later he described his reaction, "In that moment, I felt a strange sensation in my chest that made me gulp for air. This woman had literally taken my breath away."[1] On the surface, the romance didn't seem so unlikely, but what 19-year-old Camille Garcia didn't know was that Michael was in the "family business."

Michael had grown up as the son of Sonny Franzese, the notorious Underboss of New York's violent and feared Colombo crime family. Intelligent and ambitious, Michael took a blood oath that bound him to the mob and then began a meteoric rise in organized crime. He was quickly named a Capo (Captain) in the family, but not even that title captured his power and influence. Sometimes referred to as the "Prince of the Mafia," Franzese at his most affluent generated an estimated $5 to $8 million per week from legal and illegal businesses. Fourteen law enforcement agencies poured money into a taskforce with a sole objective—bring down the sophisticated young mobster.

MICHAEL & CAMILLE
FRANZESE

"Though one may be overpowered, two can defend themselves. A cord of three strands is not quickly broken."

– ECCLESIASTES 4:12

But that one poolside encounter initiated a love that changed everything. And, the love was not just the romantic one that grew between Michael and Camille. Michael's growing love and fascination with Camille also drew him to her strong faith in Jesus. In 1985, the two wed and Michael made two vows—one to Camille and the other a courageous vow to quit the mob. Shortly afterward, he heard the message that God's love offered him forgiveness and redemption, and Michael made a decision to follow Christ.

[1] Michael Franzese, *Blood Covenant* (New Kensington, PA: Whitaker House, 2003), 180.

The relationship that might have seemed so impossible—the innocent Christian teenager and the powerful mobster—instead grew into a solid God-centered marriage. Over time, the marriage withstood challenges that would have destroyed other couples: the years Michael spent in prison, family and friends counseling Camille to leave him, and even the threats against Michael's life for breaking his blood oath to the New York mob. In the face of danger and doubt, they loved, and the marriage held firm.

Today, Michael is an author and a Christian speaker who tells his inspiring story to churches, prison and youth ministries as well as sports organizations like the NBA and others. He and his wife Camille have four children, and the couple is active in their church and other Christian ministries.

> Read more about Michael's story in his biography *Blood Covenant* as well as in *The Good, the Bad and the Forgiven*, available from Outreach Publishing in 2008.

DISCUSSION

 Read Romans 5:5 and 1 John 4:19.

QUESTION 5: What do these verses teach about how and why we are able to love?

_____

_____

_____

_____

_____

 Read Philippians 2:1-4.

QUESTION 6: Verses 1 and 2 of this passage are shown below. The two verses form a conditional statement that starts with "if" and continues with "then." Read through the verses carefully. What conditions start with the word "if"? What does this passage say we need to have in order to love others? In particular, what do we receive when we're united with Christ? What do we need from the Holy Spirit?

"**If** you have any encouragement from being united with Christ, **if** any comfort from his love, **if** any fellowship with the Spirit, if any tenderness and compassion, **then** make my joy complete by being like-minded, having the same love, being one in spirit and purpose." (NIV)

_____

_____

_____

_____

_____

QUESTION 7: How does Caleb's behavior in the video contrast with verses 3 and 4 in this passage?

_____

_____

_____

_____

_____

QUESTION 8: Think about John Holt's answer to his son, "You can't love her because you can't give her what you don't have." How does John's point align with this passage? What "if" condition(s) does Caleb most need in his life in order to love his wife?

_____

_____

_____

_____

_____

QUESTION 9: Think about your marriage (or other significant relationships in your life). To what degree do you try to manage the relationship using your own wisdom and abilities? What's the result?

_____

_____

_____

_____

_____

Read 1 John 4:7-19.

QUESTION 10: This passage of Scripture explains how God's love for us works in our lives. As you read through these verses, what phrases or ideas particularly touch you?

_____

_____

_____

_____

_____

QUESTION 11: What does verse 13 say God has given us to enable us to "live in Him?" Give some practical examples from your life of how you know God lives in you.

_____

_____

_____

_____

_____

Close in prayer.

FIREPROOFING APPLICATION

 ## FIREPROOFING FOR WOMEN

 Read John 3:16.

QUESTION 1: In this week's video, Caleb is missing the Source of real love in his life. The foundation for this love is described in the most famous verse in the Bible—John 3:16. How would you answer this week's burning question, "Do you know God's love, and do you reflect that love to your spouse?"

_____

_____

_____

_____

_____

Read 1 John 4:18.

QUESTION 2: God's love for us and within us is perfect. As you read this verse, is there anything you fear about fully and unconditionally loving your spouse? About loving God? Identify any fears you have, and pray for God to help you "drive out fear" with His love.

_____

_____

_____

_____

_____

QUESTION 3: This week the group discussed loving through God versus trying to love using your own strength and ability. Below are several ways in which you can love your spouse through God. Rate yourself on each question.

How frequently do you study God's word about love and marriage and use that wisdom to guide you?

|⊢————————————————————————————————⊣|

Very Infrequently   **Neutral**   **Frequently**   **Very Infrequently**   **Frequently**

When you struggle to love your spouse, how likely are you to pray for God's encouragement, strength and guidance?

|⊢————————————————————————————————⊣|

Very Unlikely   **Unlikely**   **Neutral**   **Likely**   **Very Likely**

How likely are you to ask God to help you view and love your spouse in the same way He does?

|⊢————————————————————————————————⊣|

Very Unlikely   **Unlikely**   **Neutral**   **Likely**   **Very Likely**

How frequently do you pray for your spouse?

|⊢————————————————————————————————⊣|

Very Infrequently   **Neutral**   **Frequently**   **Very Infrequently**   **Frequently**

FIREPROOFING CHALLENGE FOR THE WEEK
There are two options for the *Fireproofing Challenge* this week.

OPTION 1: If you haven't already entered into a lifelong relationship with God, do it now; you can then use His great love to support a lasting marriage. God's love doesn't require perfection or complicated steps. Although sin separates us from God, God has made a way for us. Jesus came to bridge the gap between a perfect God and imperfect mankind. As the Bible states it:

"If you confess with your mouth the Lord Jesus and believe in your heart that God has raised Him from the dead, you will be saved."
–ROMANS 10:9

That's all it takes—just an acknowledgement of your sins, your need for God's love and the sacrifice Jesus made for you. If made with a sincere and open heart, this confession will bring God's presence into your soul and give you eternal life with your Creator.

If you want to receive this gift of love from God, simply pray a prayer like this:

Dear Jesus,

I don't know why you love me so much that you were willing to die a terrible death just for me. But I know that you did it so my sins could be forgiven and I could enter into a relationship with God. I know that I have sinned against you and that my sins separate me from you. I am truly sorry—please forgive me. Help me avoid temptation and sin as I follow after you. Thank you for loving me and dying for me. I offer my life to you today, Jesus, and turn the reins over to you. Thank you for your sacrifice, and for allowing me to know your perfect love. Amen.

If you prayed this prayer, tell your spouse (and the group if you are going through *Fireproof Your Marriage* in a small group setting.)

OPTION 2: If you already have a committed relationship with Jesus, then you have His love and the Holy Spirit to help you love your spouse.

Look at your answers in question 3. Select the lowest-ranked question and for the rest of the week focus on improvements you can make in this area. Pray for your spouse and about the areas in which you could improve.

 FIREPROOFING FOR MEN

 Read John 3:16.

QUESTION 1: In this week's video, what Caleb is missing is the Source for real love. The foundation for this love is described in the most famous verse in the Bible—John 3:16. How would you answer this week's burning question, "Do you know God's love, and are you reflecting that love to your spouse?"

_____

_____

_____

_____

 **Read John 4:18.**

QUESTION 2: God's love for us and within us is perfect. As you read this verse, is there anything you fear about fully and unconditionally loving your spouse? About loving God? Identify any fears you have, and pray for God to help you "drive out fear" with His love.

_____

_____

_____

_____

_____

QUESTION 3: This week the group discussed loving through God versus trying to love using your own strength and ability. Below are several ways in which you can love your spouse through God. Rate yourself on each question.

How frequently do you study God's word about love and marriage and use that wisdom to guide you?

Very Infrequently   Neutral   Frequently   Very Infrequently   Frequently

When you struggle to love your spouse, how likely are you to pray for God's encouragement, strength and guidance?

Very Unlikely   Unlikely   Neutral   Likely   Very Likely

How likely are you to ask God to help you view and love your spouse in the same way He does?

Very Unlikely   Unlikely   Neutral   Likely   Very Likely

How frequently do you pray for your spouse?

Very Infrequently   Neutral   Frequently   Very Infrequently   Frequently

FIREPROOFING CHALLENGE FOR THE WEEK

There are two options for the *Fireproofing Challenge* this week.

OPTION 1: If you haven't already entered into a lifelong relationship with God, do it now; you can then use His great love to support a lasting marriage. God's love doesn't require perfection or complicated steps. Although sin separates us from God, God has made a way for us. Jesus came to bridge the gap between a perfect God and imperfect mankind. As the Bible states it:

"If you confess with your mouth the Lord Jesus and believe in your heart that God has raised Him from the dead, you will be saved."
–ROMANS 10:9

That's all it takes—just an acknowledgement of your sins, your need for God's love and the sacrifice Jesus made for you. If made with a sincere and open heart, this confession will bring God's presence into your soul and give you eternal life with your Creator.

If you want to receive this gift of love from God, simply pray a prayer like this:

Dear Jesus,
I don't know why you love me so much that you were willing to die a terrible death just for me. But I know that you did it so my sins could be forgiven and I could enter into a relationship with God. I know that I have sinned against you and that my sins separate me from you. I am truly sorry—please forgive me. Help me avoid temptation and sin as I follow after you. Thank you for loving me and dying for me. I offer my life to you today, Jesus, and turn the reins over to you. Thank you for your sacrifice, and for allowing me to know your perfect love. Amen.

If you prayed this prayer, tell your spouse (and the group if you are going through *Fireproof Your Marriage* in a small group setting.)

OPTION 2: If you already have a committed relationship with Jesus, then you have His love and the Holy Spirit to help you love your spouse.

Look at your answers in question 3. Select the lowest-ranked question and for the rest of the week focus on improvements you can make in this area. Pray for your spouse and about the areas in which you could improve.

FIREPROOFING FOR COUPLES

Open your time together with prayer, asking God to give you wisdom as well as a receptive heart and mind.

 Read 1 John 4:7-19 together.

QUESTION 1: In what ways do you follow the teachings in this passage in regard to your spouse? In what ways do you struggle to love each other as God first loved you?

_____

_____

_____

_____

_____

QUESTION 2: Review your ratings from question 3 in the *Fireproofing for Women/Men* section. Discuss the reasons for each and how you might improve any low ratings.

_____

_____

_____

_____

QUESTION 3: Share the one step you are taking (from the *Fireproofing Challenge* section) to love each other better. If you made a decision to accept God's love through His Son Jesus, share that news with your spouse.

_____

_____

_____

_____

Close in prayer.

"*For this reason a man will leave his father and mother and be united to his wife, and the two will become one flesh. So they are no longer two, but one. Therefore what God has joined together let man not separate.*"

– MATTHEW 19:5-6

SESSION 3:
Love for a Lifetime

Open in prayer.

 ## THE BURNING QUESTION

Do you understand the "covenant" nature of marriage vows?

 ## FIREPROOF VIDEO

Watch the **SESSION 3** video clip on your *Fireproof Your Marriage* DVD.

 ## DISCUSSION

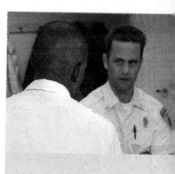

QUESTION 1: What differences do you observe in how Caleb and Michael view marriage vows?

_____

_____

_____

_____

_____

_____

_____

> *"Catherine and I were in love when we got married. But, today we're two very different people. It's just not working out anymore."*
>
> – CALEB HOLT
> IN *FIREPROOF*

QUESTION 2: The emotions surrounding a difficult marriage can be very strong; partners sometimes rationalize and defend a poor decision. As Caleb talks with Michael, how does he explain the pending divorce? Write down the reasons he gives.

_____

_____

_____

_____

_____

QUESTION 3: Michael tells Caleb, "I've seen you run into a burning building to save people you don't even know, but you're going to let your own marriage burn to the ground." Why do you think some people work through their marriage problems but others do not?

_____

_____

_____

_____

_____

 FIREPROOF ILLUSTRATION

 Read the following section either quietly to yourself as you prepare for your weekly session or aloud during the discussion time with your small group or spouse.

FOR BETTER OR FOR WORSE

"Two are better than one." – ECCLESIASTES 4:9

Long ago, Israel's King Solomon handed down both wisdom and poetry on the topic of marriage. We all understand "two are better than one" when we long for a best friend, lover and ally who will remain with us for the rest of our life. Solomon captured the feelings eloquently when he wrote, _"This is my lover, this is my friend."_ (Song of Solomon 5:16) In the same book of the Bible, Solomon also invites his beautiful wife to "come with me." His words are frequently used in weddings because we can easily identify with the romance and desire for a "soulmate."

The vast majority of adults find someone to fill their need for a partner and companion—approximately 90% will eventually marry. Unfortunately, around half of all marriages end in divorce. Most perish from what's called "irreconcilable differences," which is a catch-all phrase for Caleb's description, "It's just not working out anymore." Other common explanations include, "I've fallen out of love with him/her," or, "We're just two different people now."

In reality, there are days in every relationship when there are "irreconcilable differences." But God intended marriage to last a lifetime. The salt and pepper lesson portrays a great truth—marriage is a *covenant*. The dictionary defines "covenant" as a solemn agreement with legal validity. In our culture, however, marriage is sometimes treated more like a 50/50 contract—spouses do their part IF they feel the other partner is doing his/her part.

"Do you know what that ring on your finger means? It means that you made a lifelong covenant—you putting on that ring while saying your vows. The sad part about it is when most people say, 'for better or for worse,' they really only mean for the better."

– MICHAEL SIMMONS
IN *FIREPROOF*

 DISCUSSION

Read Matthew 19:5-6.

QUESTION 4: What word or phrase does Jesus use to describe marriage?

_____

_____

_____

_____

_____

...ael warns Caleb not to try to pull apart the salt and
...saying that he will break one or both of them. What are
...life consequences of divorce?

_____

_____

_____

_____

_____

QUESTION 6: Jesus says that man is not to
separate what God has joined together. In the movie
Fireproof, some of Catherine's friends blame Caleb
for the problems in their marriage. Catherine
also becomes very close to a male doctor at
the hospital where she works. List some ways
in which people can "separate" (i.e. physically,
emotionally, spiritually) a married couple.

_____

_____

_____

_____

_____

Read Malachi 2:14-16.

QUESTION 7: This passage refers to divorce as "breaking faith" (NIV).
The King James Version uses the phrase "dealt treacherously," which
means to not take vows seriously. What does this say about how God
views divorce?

_____

_____

_____

_____

_____

QUESTION 8: Verse 16 says that God hates divorce. What do you think some of the reasons might be?

_____

_____

_____

_____

_____

QUESTION 9: Look at verse 16 carefully. Is there a distinction between "God hates divorce" and "God hates *people who* divorce?" Explain your answer.

_____

_____

_____

_____

_____

Read Ecclesiastes 5:4-5.

QUESTION 10: What direction is given in this passage? How would it apply to marriage?

_____

_____

_____

_____

_____

QUESTION 11: How does this principle differ from the world's view of a covenant relationship, i.e. is it contingent on both parties fulfilling their obligations?

_____

_____

_____

_____

Close in prayer.

FIREPROOFING APPLICATION

FIREPROOFING FOR WOMEN

 Re-read Ecclesiastes 5:4-5.

QUESTION 1: When you first got married, how solemn and permanent did you consider your vows? How fully did you understand the nature of a covenant? (Note: If you are not yet married, answer this question in light of how you view future wedding vows.)

_____

_____

_____

_____

_____

QUESTION 2: Some traditional wedding vows are listed below. Rate how well you feel you've kept each vow in your marriage (with 1 being the lowest rating and 10 the highest.) If you wrote your own vows or used something different, substitute those vows as you answer the questions. If you are not yet married, rate yourself on how well you understand and are committed to the vow.

To have and to hold (how well have you bonded and "held" to your husband)

1   2   3   4   5   6   7   8   9   10

For better or worse (how stable is your treatment of your husband, regardless of circumstances?)

1   2   3   4   5   6   7   8   9   10

For richer or poorer (how well does your marriage stand up to financial pressures?)

1   **2**   **3**   **4**   **5**   **6**   **7**   **8**   **9**   **10**

In sickness and in health (is your marriage affected by health struggles?)

1   **2**   **3**   **4**   **5**   **6**   **7**   **8**   **9**   **10**

To love and to cherish (refer to your accomplishment of the principles in Ephesians 5 from last session)

1   **2**   **3**   **4**   **5**   **6**   **7**   **8**   **9**   **10**

I pledge my faithfulness (are you faithful to your husband?)

1   **2**   **3**   **4**   **5**   **6**   **7**   **8**   **9**   **10**

Re-read Matthew 19:5-6.

QUESTION 3: Is there anything or anyone that "separates" you from your husband? What one step can you take this week to address the issue?

_____

_____

_____

_____

_____

FIREPROOFING CHALLENGE FOR THE WEEK
Select the vow to which you gave the lowest rating. Identify the key reason(s) for the rating. What can you begin to do to improve that rating? (For example: expressing your love for your husband in a clear manner, resolving financial issues and/or trusting them to God, being completely faithful...) Write down one key step and begin to practice it this week.

FIREPROOFING FOR MEN

Re-read Ecclesiastes 5:4-5.

QUESTION 1: When you first got married, how solemn and permanent did you consider your vows? How fully did you understand the nature of a covenant? (Note: If you are not yet married, answer this question in light of how you view future wedding vows.)

_____

_____

_____

_____

_____

QUESTION 2: Some traditional wedding vows are listed below. Rate how well you feel you've kept each vow in your marriage (with 1 being the lowest rating and 10 the highest.) If you wrote your own vows or used something different, substitute those vows as you answer the questions. If you are not yet married, rate yourself on how well you understand and are committed to the vow.

To have and to hold (how well have you bonded and "held" to your wife?)

1   2   3   4   5   6   7   8   9   10

For better or worse (how stable is your treatment of your wife, regardless of circumstances?)

1   2   3   4   5   6   7   8   9   10

For richer or poorer (how well does your marriage stand up to financial pressures?)

1   2   3   4   5   6   7   8   9   10

In sickness and in health (is your marriage affected by health struggles?)

1   2   3   4   5   6   7   8   9   10

To love and to cherish (refer to your accomplishment of the principles in Ephesians 5 from last session)

1	2	3	4	5	6	7	8	9	10

I pledge my faithfulness (are you faithful to your wife?)

1	2	3	4	5	6	7	8	9	10

 Re-read Matthew 19:5-6.

QUESTION 3: Is there anything or anyone that "separates" you from your wife? What one step can you take this week to address the issue?

_____

_____

_____

_____

FIREPROOFING CHALLENGE FOR THE WEEK
Select the vow to which you gave the lowest rating. Identify the key reason(s) for the rating. What can you begin to do to improve that rating? (For example: expressing your love for your wife in a clear manner, resolving financial issues and/or trusting them to God, being completely faithful...) Write down one key step and begin to practice it this week.

 FIREPROOFING FOR COUPLES

Open your time together with prayer, asking God to give you wisdom as well as a receptive heart and mind.

 Read Matthew 19:5-6 together.

QUESTION 1: Together, list the ways in which you feel you have become "one flesh." How are your lives and hearts intertwined?

_____

_____

_____

_____

_____

QUESTION 2: Review your answers to the marriage vow ratings. Do any of your spouse's answers surprise you? Do you disagree with any of them? Discuss the reasons for each rating, affirm high marks and talk about how you might improve any low ones.

_____

_____

_____

_____

_____

QUESTION 3: Share the one step you will take (from the _Fireproofing Challenge_ section) to better fulfill your marriage vows.

_____

_____

_____

_____

_____

FIREPROOFING COUPLES CHALLENGE FOR THE WEEK
This week, there is a special _Fireproofing Challenge_; this one is designed to be completed as a couple

Consider renewing your vows to each other. You can do this privately, in a ceremony with the other couples in your group, or even in a larger ceremony sponsored by your church. You might also want to write your own vows to help capture what you will commit to each other for the rest of your marriage.

Close in prayer.

"No temptation has seized you except what is
common to man. And God is faithful; he will not
let you be tempted beyond what you can bear.
But when you are tempted, he will also provide
a way out so that you can stand up under it."

– 1 CORINTHIANS 10:13

SESSION 4:
Breaking Free

Open in prayer.

 THE BURNING QUESTION

Are temptations or addictions threatening your marriage?

 FIREPROOF VIDEO

Watch the **SESSION 4** video clip on your *Fireproof Your Marriage* DVD.

 DISCUSSION

The topics of temptation and addiction can be awkward and difficult to discuss. This week, we recommend that you break into two separate groups—men in one group and women in another. Same-sex groups encourage honest discussion and create a more comfortable atmosphere for difficult conversation.

"Submit yourselves, then, to God. Resist the devil, and he will flee from you."

– JAMES 4:7

Rule of Engagement: The *How to Use This Guide* section
some suggested guidelines for small groups. As you go
cussion, remember to keep everything you hear confidential.
Also ____ ers with gentleness and respect, and do not give advice that
isn't spe ____ cally solicited.

If a sensitive issue involves your spouse, and discussing it would embarrass
or devalue them in the eyes of the group, save that discussion for the
Fireproofing for Couples time later this week.

Read through *How to Use This Guide* section if you have questions about
how best to participate in the discussion.

QUESTION 1: Just as Caleb has made a decision to follow God and restore
his marriage, he is confronted with temptation. Have you found this pattern
to be true in your life—does temptation sometimes appear unexpectedly?
Explain and give examples.

_____

_____

_____

_____

_____

QUESTION 2: In this scene, Caleb walks away from the computer and
picks up *The Love Dare* book. How does the lesson in the book encourage
him to resist temptation? What specifically was helpful?

_____

_____

_____

_____

_____

FIREPROOF ILLUSTRATION

 Read the following section either quietly to yourself as you prepare for your weekly session or aloud during the discussion time with your small group or spouse.

PARASITES

In the video clip, Caleb reads this lesson in *The Love Dare*:

> *"Watch out for parasites. A parasite is anything that latches onto you or your partner and sucks the life out of your marriage. They're normally in the form of addictions like gambling, drugs or pornography. They promise pleasure but grow like a disease and consume more and more of your thoughts, time and money. They steal away your loyalty and your heart from those you love. Marriages rarely survive if parasites are present.*
>
> *If you love your wife, you must destroy any addiction that has your heart. If you don't, it will destroy you."*

There are many "parasites" that can threaten and eventually destroy marriages. Consider the following list:

Adultery	**Pornography**	**Alcoholism**
Eating Disorders	**Gambling**	**Drug Addiction**
Internet-based Addictions	**Overeating**	

PORNOGRAPHY BY THE NUMBERS:

2006 worldwide revenue for the pornography industry	$97 Billion
Average number of visitors per month to adult web sites (worldwide)	72 Million
Percentage of men ages 18 to 34 who visit a pornographic site in a typical month	More than 70%
Percentage of Internet pornography that involves children	20%
Divorces in which excessive online pornography was a factor	More than 50%
Percentage of families saying pornography is a factor in their home	47%
Average age of first Internet exposure to pornography	11 years old
Percentage of children ages 8 to 16 who have viewed online pornography (most unintentionally while doing homework)	90%

The Bible says this about temptation, sin and consequences:

> "When tempted, no one should say, 'God is tempting me.' For God cannot be tempted by evil, nor does he tempt anyone; but each one is tempted when, by his own evil desire, he is dragged away and enticed. Then, after desire has conceived, it gives birth to sin; and sin, when it is full-grown, gives birth to death." – JAMES 1:13-15

The pattern of temptation looks like this:

| TEMPTATION | SINFUL THOUGHTS | SINFUL ACTIONS | CONSEQUENCES |

Consequences include guilty feelings, damaged or destroyed relationships, financial loss, divorce or the loss of our reputation, home, job or friends. It's a very sobering thought, but God does not intend for us to hopelessly fall victim to temptation. Read what the Apostle Paul wrote in his letter to the Romans:

> "So I find this law at work: When I want to do good, evil is right there with me. For in my inner being I delight in God's law; but I see another law at work in the members of my body, waging war against the law of my mind and making me a prisoner of the law of sin at work within my members. What a wretched man I am! Who will rescue me from this body of death? Thanks be to God—through Jesus Christ our Lord!" – ROMANS 7:21-25

Paul eloquently expresses our dilemma: wanting to obey God, yet struggling with temptation and sin. This passage also points out the ultimate solution—victory and salvation through Jesus Christ! God has a plan to strengthen us and rescue us from sin and death.

 DISCUSSION

 Read 1 Peter 5:8-9.

QUESTION 3: What do these verses say about the likelihood that we will face temptation?

_____

_____

_____

_____

QUESTION 4: According to this Scripture, how should we protect ourselves from temptation and sin?

_____

_____

_____

_____

Read Matthew 5:27-30.

QUESTION 5: What does Jesus say about our actions, our thoughts and the heart? How does this passage apply to the example in this week's video clip—Caleb being tempted by pornography?

_____

_____

_____

_____

Read 1 Corinthians 6:18-20 and 2 Timothy 2:22.

QUESTION 6: We've already discussed the importance of removing the source of temptation from our lives. These passages suggest another method of dealing with temptation: what is it? Give some practical examples of "fleeing" from immorality.

_____

_____

_____

_____

_____

QUESTION 7: Under what conditions would it be more effective to remove the temptation? When would it be better to remove yourself?

_____

_____

_____

_____

_____

 Read Psalm 119:9-11.

QUESTION 8: How does studying the Bible fit into a strategy for resisting sin?

_____

_____

_____

_____

_____

 Read Hebrews 4:15.

QUESTION 9: Why is Jesus able to understand the temptations that face us? Does this comfort you in your struggle? Why or why not? What example does Jesus provide for us?

_____

_____

_____

_____

_____

 Read 1 Corinthians 10:13.

QUESTION 10: What promise does God make in regard to temptation in this verse? How can you use this promise to help when you are tempted?

_____

_____

_____

_____

_____

Read 1 John 1:9.

QUESTION 11: When we "confess", we agree with God regarding our thoughts and behavior. What does God promise in return when we confess our sin?

_____

_____

_____

_____

_____

Read James 5:16.

QUESTION 12: When we draw together as Christ's church, we receive strength and encouragement from each other. What does this passage also teach about the effect of confessing to each other? How does this help us resist temptation and turn away from sin?

_____

_____

_____

_____

_____

Close in prayer.

FIREPROOFING APPLICATION

 ## FIREPROOFING FOR WOMEN

 Read James 1:13-15.

QUESTION 1: Which of the following do you find yourself doing in response to temptation?

❑ Rationalizing, (i.e. "It's just this one time," "God will forgive me," "I deserve this," or, "It's OK for me to do this because...")

❑ Hiding your behavior

❑ Suffering from guilt

❑ Withdrawing from God

 Read James 4:7.

QUESTION 2: Read through the list below. Which of these particularly help you resist temptation? Which of them do you regularly use? Give some examples where appropriate.

❑ Reading the Bible

❑ Praying

❑ Talking about the issue with other people

❑ Confessing to God

❑ Leaving the place where the temptation occurred

❑ Immediately getting involved with another activity

❑ Going to a place where you are with other people

❑ Going to church, or participating in a church activity

❑ Other: _____

 Re-read James 5:16.

QUESTION 3: Some "parasites" are the type we can fall into over and over again. This type of sin or temptation might require an accountability group or partner—a person or body of believers who can help you consistently turn away from sinful thoughts or actions. You can find accountability and strength in a trustworthy friend, a professional counselor or a support group or organization. If you don't already have someone like this in your life, pray that God will reveal that person or group to you.

_____

_____

_____

_____

FIREPROOFING CHALLENGE OF THE WEEK
Make sure you are in a quiet place with some time available for prayer.

 Read Psalm 139:23-24.

In this passage, King David prays for God to search his heart and, "see if there is any offensive way in me." (NIV) Pray a similar prayer, asking God to search your heart and your ways and reveal any "parasites" or potential threats to your marriage. Remember the definition of a parasite from the discussion portion of this session. A parasite:

- Latches on to you or your partner
- Sucks the life out of your marriage
- Promises pleasure, but grows like a disease
- Consumes more and more of your thoughts, time and money
- Steals away your heart from those you love

As you pray, quiet your thoughts and listen, letting your heart be open to God's answer. Honestly consider what God brings to your mind. As you become aware of any parasites in your life, take these steps:

1. Confess the sin to God.
2. Pray about ways in which you can resist or flee from that temptation. Look at the list in question 2. Is there anything on the list that could help you that you aren't currently doing? This week, take one step that will help you resist a specific temptation.
3. Prayerfully consider confessing the sin to your spouse and/or to a trusted friend.

FIREPROOFING FOR MEN

 Read James 1:13-15.

QUESTION 1: Which of the following do you find yourself doing in response to temptation?

❏ Rationalizing, (i.e. "It's just this one time," "God will forgive me," "I deserve this," or, "It's OK for me to do this because..."

❏ Hiding your behavior

❏ Suffering from guilt

❏ Withdrawing from God

 Read James 4:7.

QUESTION 2: Read through the list below. Which of these particularly help you resist temptation? Which of them do you regularly use? Give some examples where appropriate.

❏ Reading the Bible

❏ Praying

❏ Talking about the issue with other people

❏ Confessing to God

❏ Leaving the place where the temptation occurred

❏ Immediately getting involved with another activity

❏ Going to a place where you are with other people

❏ Going to church, or participating in a church activity

❏ Other: _____

 Re-read James 5:16.

QUESTION 3: Some "parasites" are the type we can fall into over and over again. This type of sin or temptation might require an accountability group or partner—a person or body of believers who can help you consistently turn away from sinful thoughts or actions. You can find accountability and strength in a trustworthy friend, a professional counselor or a support group or organization. If you don't already have someone like this in your life, pray that God will reveal that person or group to you.

_____

_____

_____

_____

FIREPROOFING CHALLENGE OF THE WEEK
Make sure you are in a quiet place with some time available for prayer.

 Read Psalm 139:23-24.

In this passage, King David prays for God to search his heart and, *"see if there is any offensive way in me."* (NIV) Pray a similar prayer, asking God to search your heart and your ways and reveal any "parasites" or potential threats to your marriage. Remember the definition of a parasite from the discussion portion of this session. A parasite:

- Latches on to you or your partner
- Sucks the life out of your marriage
- Promises pleasure, but grows like a disease
- Consumes more and more of your thoughts, time and money
- Steals away your heart from those you love

As you pray, quiet your thoughts and listen, letting your heart be open to God's answer. Honestly consider what God brings to your mind. As you become aware of any parasites in your life, take these steps:

1. Confess the sin to God.
2. Pray about ways in which you can resist or flee from that temptation. Look at the list in question 2. Is there anything on the list that could help you that you aren't currently doing? This week, take one step that will help you resist a specific temptation.
3. Prayerfully consider confessing the sin to your spouse and/or to a trusted friend.

FIREPROOFING FOR COUPLES

Open your time together with prayer, asking God to give you wisdom as well as a receptive heart and mind.

 Together, read Ecclesiastes 4:9-12.

Consider the teaching in this passage as you go through the next three questions.

QUESTION 1: Share your answers to question 1 in the *Fireproofing for Men/Women* section. How do you each struggle with temptation? Are there ways in which you can encourage each other and provide both understanding and accountability?

_____

_____

_____

_____

QUESTION 2: Share your answers to question 2 in the *Fireproofing for Men/Women* section. As you review the ways that help you resist sin and temptation, are there any you can do together? How can you encourage or strengthen your spouse as he/she follows those steps?

_____

_____

_____

_____

QUESTION 3: Share any insights you each received from your *Fireproofing Challenge*. As you feel led, confess to your spouse any sins God revealed during your prayer time. Tell your mate the step(s) you're taking to resist/flee temptation. Think about the passage from Ecclesiastes—how can you "help each other up" and defend yourselves against Satan's schemes? How is God the "third strand" in the strong cord of your marriage?

_____

_____

_____

Close in prayer.

Be kind and compassionate to one another,
forgiving each other,
just as in Christ God forgave you.

– EPHESIANS 4:32

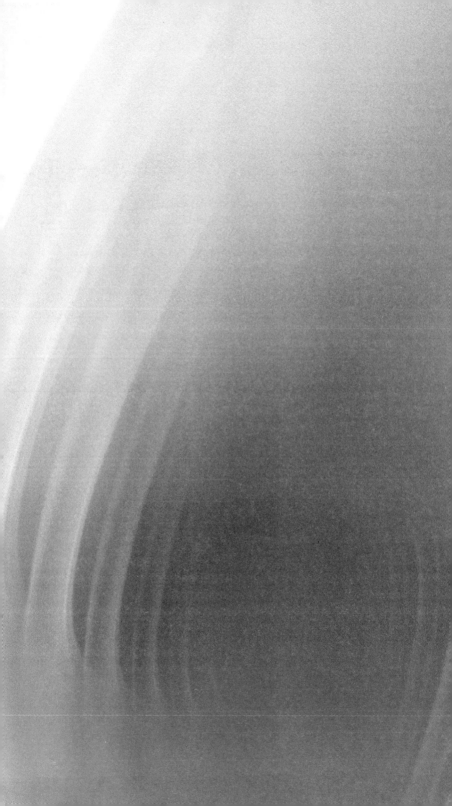

SESSION 5:
Forgiveness

Open in prayer.

 THE BURNING QUESTION

Is unforgiveness hindering your relationship with God or with your spouse? Is there anything for which you need to ask forgiveness?

 FIREPROOF VIDEO

Watch the **SESSION 5** video clip on your *Fireproof Your Marriage* DVD.

 DISCUSSION

QUESTION 1: As you watched this scene, what touched you the most? Why?

_____

_____

_____

_____

_____

Read Colossians 3:12-15.

QUESTION 2: This passage gives wisdom for healthy relationships. List some ways in which Caleb illustrated this passage. How did he show compassion, kindness, humility, gentleness, patience and a desire for peace?

_____

_____

_____

_____

_____

 Read Ephesians 4:15.

QUESTION 3: How does Caleb "confess" to Catherine and speak the truth about his past treatment of her? If he had been less open and honest, how do you think it would have changed the impact of his apology?

_____

_____

_____

_____

_____

_____

_____

"I am hoping—I am praying, that somehow you would be able to forgive me too."

– CALEB HOLT,
IN *FIREPROOF*

 Read Proverbs 15:1.

QUESTION 4: In earlier scenes from *Fireproof*, Caleb co
Catherine and how she treated him. During his apolog,
bring up any of Catherine's faults, nor does he blame her. W
is this significant? In what ways might her reaction have bee
if he had?

_____

_____

_____

_____

_____

_____

Read Romans 5:10, Luke 23:33-34 and 1 John 1:8-9.

QUESTION 5: According to these verses, we were all sinners and even "enemies" with God before he forgave us. In the passage from Luke, Jesus forgives <u>while</u> he is being crucified! As you think about your past—your thoughts and your actions—how greatly has God forgiven you?

_____

_____

_____

_____

_____

QUESTION 6: How readily do you forgive others? Do you set any conditions for forgiveness?

_____

_____

_____

_____

_____

_____

FIREPROOF ILLUSTRATION

Read the following section either quietly to yourself as you prepare for your weekly session or aloud during the discussion time with your small group or spouse.

A MARRIAGE TRANSFORMED

JOE & ELISA RANGEL

"God has transformed the fabric of our entire family."

– JOE RANGEL

In 2000, Joe and Elisa celebrated their 14th wedding anniversary. In reality, their marriage was anything but a celebration. Joe had engaged in a series of affairs, one of them for as long as five years. He had also succumbed to an addiction to pornography, unable to resist the lure of sexually-explicit Internet sites. His only real incentive for avoiding divorce was the fear of losing his material possessions and financial stability.

Elisa, in turn, was living in her own web of lies and deceit. In her anger and despair, she had developed a $1,000 a week addiction to speed and cocaine—a habit she hid from Joe.

They were on marital "auto-pilot", co-existing as roommates with children. There was no real communication. They had each betrayed each other's trust to the highest possible degree.

The turn-around began when Elisa was invited by a neighbor to attend a church service, then a women's retreat. Over the next year, Elisa quit drugs, continued to attend the local church and developed a committed relationship with God. At the end of that time, she approached Joe and told him, "I love someone more than I love you, and that person is Jesus." Elisa even diffused Joe's fear of monetary repercussions, telling him that she wouldn't fight him for the house or their money.

As Joe tells the story, "That started the forgiveness. I confessed everything to her and then said, 'You might not be able to forgive me.'" Elisa's answer was clear, "I didn't forgive you because you earned it or you deserve it. I forgave you because God forgave me." Joe gave his life over to Christ as well, and together with Elisa decided to honor God with his life and marriage.

The transformation of their marriage hasn't always been smooth and easy. There were times when they would drive past a place where Joe had an affair, and Elisa would struggle with her emotions. "She had to dig deep," Joe explains. His behavior has changed as well. "Now, if we get into an argument, I don't 'check out.' There is no back door out of our marriage— we've sealed it shut. I honor Elisa by giving her grace that's only a shadow of God's grace for us."

Today, Joe serves God full-time in his job and plays guitar in a Christian rock band. Elisa is on staff at the church where she first came to Christ. They are both active in the church, mentoring other couples and serving in the marriage and family ministry.

 DISCUSSION

 Read Matthew 5:23-24, Matthew 6:12-15 and Mark 11:25-26.

QUESTION 7: All of these passages are Jesus' teaching on the concept of forgiveness. As you read through them, do they portray forgiveness as just a feeling or as something that requires a deliberate decision? Is there anything in the three passages that indicates forgiveness might also require action?

_____

_____

_____

_____

_____

QUESTION 8: Think of a time when you forgave someone—what did you do? How did your feelings and your actions change? Take some time to discuss what forgiveness looks like on a day-to-day basis.

_____

_____

_____

_____

_____

QUESTION 9: As you read these verses, do you see any consequences for unforgiveness? How does unforgiveness affect your relationship with God?

_____

_____

_____

_____

_____

_____

Read Philippians 1:6.

QUESTION 10: Consider this verse and how it applies to both you and your spouse. Is it up to you to cause your spouse to change, or is God able and willing to transform your mate? How can this promise change how you treat your husband/wife?

_____

_____

_____

_____

_____

FIREPROOFING APPLICATION

FIREPROOFING FOR WOMEN

 Read Matthew 18:21-35.

QUESTION 1: When someone we dearly love sins against us, it can cause deep hurt. In that type of situation, forgiveness might be an on-going process. Even when we forgive, the feelings of hurt and anger can resurface, especially if their sinful behavior occurs multiple times, or if we encounter a reminder of old wounds. (Remember the story of Elisa and Joe, and Elisa driving past a place where Joe had had an affair?) How does Jesus' answer of "seventy-seven times" apply? Is there something in your marriage that might make forgiveness take some time or be an on-going process?

_____

_____

_____

_____

_____

 Re-read Philippians 1:6.

QUESTION 2: Is there any way in which you are trying to force your spouse to change, either by your actions or your words? Would this behavior feel critical or loving to your mate? For at least this week, commit to praying for your husband and trusting in God and His ability to transform your spouse. Particularly pray about any flaw in your husband that you might have been trying to control or change on your own.

_____

_____

_____

_____

_____

QUESTION 3: Read through the list below. In your view, which of them describe what forgiveness <u>is</u> or what forgiveness <u>does</u>? Which ones are <u>sometimes</u> true of forgiveness? Which are <u>not</u> true of forgiveness? Fill in the table below by writing each list item in the appropriate column. One is shown as an example.

- Important for reducing my own stress and anger
- Deserved
- Just a feeling
- Require an apology from the person I'm forgiving
- The same as forgetting
- A step in the process of healing
- Means that I agree with the other person's behavior
- Requires that I fully trust the other person
- Minimizes the hurt I've suffered
- A deliberate decision
- Requires that the other person forgive me as well
- An on-going process
- Done in obedience to God

Forgiveness Is/Does	Forgiveness Sometimes Is/Does	Forgiveness Is Not/Does Not
Required by God		

FIREPROOFING FOR MEN

 Read Matthew 18:21-35.

QUESTION 1: When someone we dearly love sins against us, it can cause deep hurt. In that type of situation, forgiveness might be an on-going process. Even when we forgive, the feelings of hurt and anger can resurface, especially if their sinful behavior occurs multiple times, or if we encounter a reminder of old wounds. (Remember the story of Elisa and Joe, and Elisa driving past a place where Joe had had an affair?) How does Jesus' answer of "seventy-seven times" apply? Is there something in your marriage that might make forgiveness take some time or be an on-going process?

_____

_____

_____

_____

_____

 Re-read Philippians 1:6.

QUESTION 2: Is there any way in which you are trying to force your spouse to change, either by your actions or your words? Would this behavior feel critical or loving to your mate? For at least this week, commit to praying for your wife and trusting in God and His ability to transform your spouse. Particularly pray about any flaw in your wife that you might have been trying to control or change on your own.

_____

_____

_____

_____

_____

QUESTION 3: Read through the list below. In your view, which of them describe what forgiveness is or what forgiveness does? Which ones are sometimes true of forgiveness? Which are not true of forgiveness? Fill in the table on the right by writing each list item in the appropriate column. One is shown as an example.

- Important for reducing my own stress and anger
- Deserved
- Just a feeling
- Require an apology from the person I'm forgiving
- The same as forgetting
- A step in the process of healing
- Means that I agree with the other person's behavior
- Requires that I fully trust the other person
- Minimizes the hurt I've suffered
- A deliberate decision
- Requires that the other person forgive me as well
- An on-going process
- Done in obedience to God

Forgiveness Is/Does	Forgiveness Sometimes Is/Does	Forgiveness Is Not/Does Not
Required by God		

FIREPROOFING CHALLENGE FOR THE WEEK

CHALLENGE 1: Pray and ask God to reveal anything you have done to hurt or offend your spouse. First, ask for God's forgiveness. Then, commit to apologizing to your mate. Remember Caleb's example in the video clip and apologize without blaming your spouse or excusing what happened.

CHALLENGE 2: Pray and ask God to reveal anything you need to forgive. God can strengthen us and provide us with wisdom and encouragement—pray for God to support you as you forgive any deep-seated hurts. Prayerfully consider when and how you should communicate your forgiveness to your spouse.

FIREPROOFING FOR COUPLES

Open your time together with prayer, asking God to give you wisdom as well as a receptive heart and mind.

QUESTION 1: Share your answers to question 3 from *Fireproofing for Men/ Women*. Explain your answers. What aspect of forgiveness do you feel is the easiest? Which is the most difficult?

_____

_____

_____

_____

_____

QUESTION 2: Take this time to offer apologies and forgiveness, as suggested by the *Fireproofing Challenge* section.

_____

_____

_____

_____

_____

QUESTION 3: Ask your spouse this question, "Is there any way in which I can love you better?" Do this with an open heart, giving your spouse permission to share their hurts or suggest ways in which you can improve your relationship.

_____

_____

_____

_____

_____

Close in prayer.

"Love is patient, love is kind. It does not envy,
it does not boast, it is not proud.
It is not rude, it is not self-seeking, it is not easily angered,
it keeps no record of wrongs.
Love does not delight in evil but rejoices with the truth.
It always protects, always trusts, always hopes, always perseveres."

– 1 CORINTHIANS 13:4-7

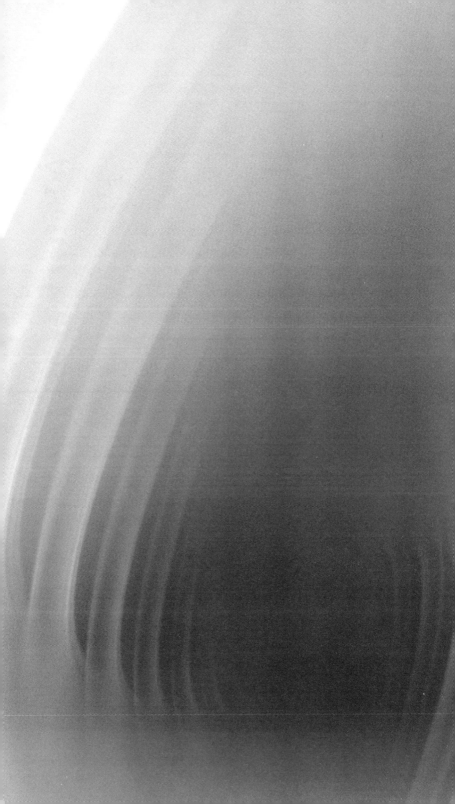

SESSION 6:
A Better Way of Loving

Open in prayer.

 ## THE BURNING QUESTION

Do you love your spouse unconditionally?

 ## FIREPROOF VIDEO

Watch the **SESSION 6** video clips on your *Fireproof Your Marriage* DVD.

SPOILER ALERT! *The final video clip for this session contains a key scene from the end of the movie. If you have not already seen* Fireproof, *you might want to skip the video portion of this session as well as the first four discussion questions; you may begin with question 5. Come back to questions 1 through 4 after you watch the movie.*

 ## DISCUSSION

QUESTION 1: In the first scene, Caleb has saved money to purchase a boat. How much money did he have put away for the boat? In the second scene, Catherine finds out that Caleb paid $24,000 to "buy medical equipment" for Catherine's mother. Why is the amount of money significant? What specifically did Caleb do?

_____

_____

_____

_____

ıw do Caleb's actions in the second scene align with this

_____ _____

_____

_____

_____

_____

QUESTION 3: At the time Caleb paid for the medical equipment, Catherine was still planning to divorce him. So there was a very real possibility Caleb would spend the money for the equipment and still wind up divorced from Catherine. Put yourself in Caleb's position— how difficult would it be for you to make that decision? In your own life, have you ever made a risky decision out of love for someone? Share the story as part of your discussion.

_____

_____

_____

_____

_____

"Above all, love each other deeply, because love covers over a multitude of sins."

– 1 PETER 4:8

QUESTION 4: One of the questions in Session 2 was, _"Who do you think is more important to Caleb, himself or his wife?"_ How did you answer that question then? How would you answer it now? If you feel that Caleb changed, what do you think caused the change?

_____

_____

_____

_____

_____

FIREPROOF ILLUSTRATION

Read the following section either quietly to yourself as you prepare for your weekly session or aloud during the discussion time with your small group or spouse.

FOR THE LOVE OF A FRIEND

The Bible has many stories of love, including the dramatic, sacrificial love of Jesus described in the New Testament gospels. The Old Testament has an amazing story of unconditional love as well, and that love existed between the unlikeliest of friends.

He was a Prince in the nation of Israel—the eldest son and heir of the first anointed King. If Jonathan looked like the Bible's description of his father Saul, then he was tall and handsome. He certainly would have met anyone's expectations for a future King. Popular with the Israelites, he was a mighty warrior—a leader in his father's armies, and known for being the first into a battle. In an account found in 1 Samuel 14, the Israelites are facing their sworn enemies, the

> *"Greater love has no one than this, that he lay down his life for his friends."*
>
> – JOHN 15:13

Philistines. Jonathan slips away from the main force, trusting in the God of his fathers to guide him as he attacks the edge of the Philistine army.

> *"Jonathan climbed up, using his hands and feet, with his armor-bearer right behind him. The Philistines fell before Jonathan, and his armor-bearer followed and killed behind him. In that first attack Jonathan and his armor-bearer killed some twenty men in an area of about half an acre."* – 1 SAMUEL 14:13-14

He was the clear heir apparent to the throne of Israel, until his father Saul turned away from God and the prophet Samuel was sent to anoint a young shepherd boy named David. The warrior Prince's response to the young David was selfless and almost inexplicable, *"Jonathan became one in spirit with David, and he loved him as himself."* (1 Samuel 18:1)

From that time on, Jonathan guarded David and honored God's choice of him as the future King. He warned David about threats from King Saul and even stood up to his father in David's defense. In an angry response, Saul chastised Jonathan and pointed out the threat David posed, *"As long as the son of Jesse lives on this earth, neither you nor your kingdom will be established."* (1 Samuel 20:31) Still, Jonathan selflessly loved the very one who would supplant him as King. *"But if my father is inclined to harm you, may the LORD deal with me, be it ever so severely, if I do not let you know and send you away safely. May the LORD be with you as he has been with my father."* (1 Samuel 20:13)

After David fled from Saul and surrounded himself with fighting men, Jonathan braved the threat from David's new army and traveled to his rival's camp to encourage him.

> *"And Saul's son Jonathan went to David at Horesh and helped him find strength in God. 'Don't be afraid,' he said. 'My father Saul will not lay a hand on you. You will be king over Israel, and I will be second to you.'"* – 1 SAMUEL 23:16-17

Jonathan was eventually slain in battle along with his father, King Saul. But, the valiant Prince's unconditional love for his friend preserved King David's life. And Jonathan's obedience to God opened the way for a covenant between the Lord and David, which was ultimately fulfilled in Jesus, the Messiah descended from the House of David.

> You can read more about Jonathan and David in 1 & 2 Samuel. Jonathan's life is also described in the historical novel, *The Prince: Jonathan* by Francine Rivers.

DISCUSSION

Read Romans 5:6-8.

QUESTION 5: This passage provides an excellent example of Jesus' unconditional love for us. As you read, did you see any conditions we must fulfill in order to be loved by God? What words, phrases or concepts touch you the most in this Scripture?

_____

_____

_____

_____

_____

QUESTION 6: In what ways can love be <u>conditional</u>? What are some conditions that people apply to loving a spouse? What are the consequences when those conditions aren't met?

_____

_____

_____

_____

_____

 Read John 13:34-35.

QUESTION 7: Does loving others sound like a suggestion? Or is the wording in this passage stronger than that? Which words in these two verses indicate how important it is that we love our spouse and others around us?

_____

_____

_____

_____

 Read John 15:9-17.

QUESTION 8: In verse 9 of this passage, Jesus tells us to "remain in my love." In what ways can we "remain in His love?" How do you think "remaining" in Jesus' love enables us to love others?

_____

_____

_____

_____

QUESTION 9: Why do you think Jesus directs us to love one another? One answer is in the previous passage, John 13:35. What are some other reasons?

_____

_____

_____

_____

QUESTION 10: Verse 13 says, _"Greater love has no one than this, that he lay down his life for his friends."_ What does Jesus mean in this verse, and is there more than one meaning? In what ways can we "lay down our lives" for one another?

_____

_____

_____

_____

Read 1 Peter 4:8.

QUESTION 11: If you love someone deeply, can that love "cover a multitude" of your own sins? Can loving another person deeply cause you to see past their sins? How so? Share an example from your own life during your discussion.

_____

_____

_____

_____

Close in prayer.

FIREPROOFING APPLICATION

FIREPROOFING FOR WOMEN

 Read 1 Corinthians 13:4-7.

QUESTION 1: Read through the story of Prince Jonathan and King David. You can also read all or parts of 1 Samuel 13 through 1 Samuel 20 for more details on their friendship. Compare Jonathan's treatment of David to the definition of love in 1 Corinthians 13:4-7. In what ways does he align with this verse?

_____

_____

_____

_____

_____

QUESTION 2: The chart below shows the description of love from 1 Corinthians 13:4-7 with each characteristic listed in the first column. In the second column, write down of a recent example of this characteristic from your own life. You can note either a time in which you DID display this characteristic (e.g. a time in which you were patient with your spouse), or you can list a time in which you did NOT display the characteristic (e.g. you "kept a record of wrongs" by reminding your mate of a past sin while in the midst of an argument.) Pick an example that helps you best understand how well you're doing at following this definition of love from 1 Corinthians 13.

CHARACTERISTIC OF LOVE	RECENT EXAMPLE FROM MY LIFE
Patience	
Kindness	
Does Not Envy	
Does Not Boast	

CHARACTERISTIC OF LOVE	RECENT EXAMPLE FROM MY LIFE
Is Not Proud	
Is Not Rude	
Is Not Self-Seeking	
Is Not Easily Angered	
Keeps No Record of Wrongs	
Does Not Delight in Evil	
Rejoices With the Truth	
Protects	
Trusts	
Hopes	
Perseveres	

FIREPROOFING CHALLENGE FOR THE WEEK
The passage from 1 Corinthians tells us that love is, "not self-seeking." That's a tough one, because as humans we are sinful and tend to focus on our own needs. This week your *Fireproofing Challenge* is to love your mate in a way that is not self-seeking. For a full week, focus on putting your mate first. Each time you make a decision that affects your spouse, set aside your needs and make the choice that is best for your mate. Pray for God to give you guidance and encouragement in this area. You might even want to find a good way to remind yourself of this *Fireproofing Challenge*; you could wear a colorful wristband during the day, or you could post a note in an area where you will see it frequently.

FIREPROOFING FOR MEN

 Read 1 Corinthians 13:4-7.

QUESTION 1: Read through the story of Prince Jonathan and King David. You can also read all or parts of 1 Samuel 13 through 1 Samuel 20 for more details on their friendship. Compare Jonathan's treatment of David to the definition of love in 1 Corinthians 13:4-7. In what ways does he align with this verse?

_____

_____

_____

_____

_____

QUESTION 2: The chart below shows the description of love from 1 Corinthians 13:4-7, with each characteristic listed in the first column. In the second column, write down of a recent example of this characteristic from your own life. You can note either a time in which you DID display this characteristic (e.g. a time in which you were patient with your spouse), or you can list a time in which you did NOT display the characteristic (e.g. you "kept a record of wrongs" by reminding your mate of a past sin while in the midst of an argument.) Pick an example that helps you best understand how well you're doing at following this definition of love from 1 Corinthians 13.

CHARACTERISTIC OF LOVE	RECENT EXAMPLE FROM MY LIFE
Patience	
Kindness	
Does Not Envy	
Does Not Boast	
Is Not Proud	
Is Not Rude	

CHARACTERISTIC OF LOVE	RECENT EXAMPLE FROM MY LIFE
Is Not Self-Seeking	
Is Not Easily Angered	
Keeps No Record of Wrongs	
Does Not Delight in Evil	
Rejoices With the Truth	
Protects	
Trusts	
Hopes	
Perseveres	

FIREPROOFING CHALLENGE FOR THE WEEK
The passage from 1 Corinthians tells us that love is, "not self-seeking." That's a tough one, because as humans we are sinful and tend to focus on our own needs. This week your *Fireproofing Challenge* is to love your mate in a way that is not self-seeking. For a full week, focus on putting your mate first. Each time you make a decision that affects your spouse, set aside your needs and make the choice that is best for your mate. Pray for God to give you guidance and encouragement in this area. You might even want to find a good way to remind yourself of your *Fireproofing Challenge;* you could wear a colorful wristband during the day, or you could post a note in an area where you will see it frequently.

FIREPROOFING FOR COUPLES

Open your time together with prayer, asking God to give you wisdom as well as a receptive heart and mind.

 Read 1 Corinthians 13:4-7 together.

QUESTION 1: Which of these characteristics have you found easiest to follow? Which have you most struggled with?

_____

_____

_____

_____

_____

QUESTION 2: Review your answers from question 2 in the *Fireproofing for Women/Men* section. Pick out a few of the answers you feel are the most significant and discuss them. If there are characteristics you feel describe your spouse's treatment of you, tell them. For example, if your mate is very good at showing you trust, let him/her know how that makes you feel loved.

_____

_____

_____

_____

_____

QUESTION 3: At the end of the week, talk about your experience with the *Fireproofing Challenge*. How did it impact your relationship this week?

_____

_____

_____

_____

Close in prayer.

NOTES

ACKNOWLEDGEMENTS

Fireproof Your Marriage is based on the movie *Fireproof* from Sherwood Pictures, Provident Films and Sony Pictures Home Entertainment. We would like to thank them for their contribution to this study and for all of the dedication and hard work they put into making the movie.

We would particularly like to acknowledge the team at Sherwood for the vision they had to reach people for Christ and to strengthen and save marriages. This study would not be possible without their love for God, their heart for others and the time and effort they put into an inspiring film.

The *Fireproof Your Marriage* curriculum contains concepts and text from Bible studies written by Michael Catt and Stephen Kendrick. We appreciate their inspiration and insight.

We would also like to thank:

- Joe and Elisa Rangel, and Michael and Cammy Franzese, for their willingness to share their personal stories.

- Craig Trevithick for developing the *Fireproof Your Marriage* DVD.

- Alex Rozga for designing the *Fireproof Your Marriage* artwork.

Finally, we are deeply grateful to God for making all things possible and for first loving us.

Fireproof Your Marriage Leader's Kit

INCLUDES: 6-session DVD, a Leader's Guide and Participant's Guide

GREAT FOR COUPLES' SMALL GROUPS

USE AS A SIX-WEEK SUNDAY SCHOOL CURRICULUM

EXCELLENT FOR A WEEKEND MARRIAGE SEMINAR

KIT INCLUDES:

DVD featuring an easy-to-follow menu, videos for each of the six sessions and extras like behind-the-scenes footage

Leader's Guide with leadership tips, group guidelines and notes for each of the sessions

Participant's Guide

Look for the *Fireproof Your Marriage* Leader's Kit at your local Christian bookstore or visit **Outreach.com** for bulk quantities.

ISBN 13: 978-0-978-71538-0
FIREPROOF © 2008 Sony Pictures Home Entertainment Inc. All Rights Reserved.

Additional *Fireproof* Resources Available From **OUTREACH**

Fireproof Your Marriage
Couple's Kit

INCLUDES: 6-session DVD and
Two Participant's Guides

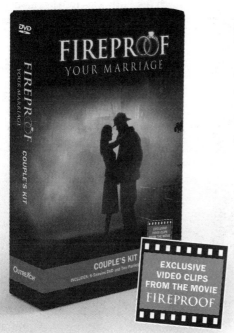

**AN IN-HOME STUDY FOR
YOU AND YOUR SPOUSE**

**GREAT AS A WEDDING
OR ANNIVERSARY GIFT**

**USE WITH PRE-MARITAL
COUNSELING**

KIT INCLUDES:

DVD featuring an easy-to-follow menu, videos for each of the six sessions and extras like behind-the-scenes footage

Two Participant's Guides

Look for the *Fireproof Your Marriage* Couple's Kit at your local Christian bookstore or visit **Outreach.com** for bulk quantities.

ISBN 13: 978-0-978-71537-3
FIREPROOF © 2008 Sony Pictures Home Entertainment Inc. All Rights Reserved.

Additional *Fireproof* Resources Available From **OUTREACH**

Fireproof Your Marriage Outreach Booklet

Share the message of God's love with a *Fireproof Your Marriage* Outreach Booklet!

Marriages both inside and outside the church are hurting. Almost everyone has felt the impact of divorce, either in their personal lives or in the lives of friends, neighbors or family. The *Fireproof Your Marriage* Outreach Booklet uses the Bible-centered themes from the movie Fireproof to provide encouragement and the hope of a life, and a marriage, changed through God's love.

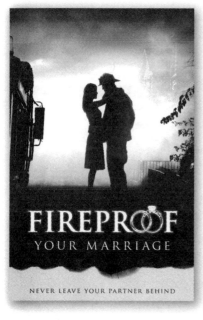

USE FIREPROOF YOUR MARRIAGE OUTREACH BOOKLETS:

- As an invitation to your church or small group

- To reach friends, family members or neighbors for Christ

- To distribute in neighborhoods or in local businesses

- As an evangelistic handout after *Fireproof* movie events or marriage seminars

Each booklet features eye-catching movie graphics, marriage help and an evangelistic message. The back cover has a place for you to add information about your church or small group.

Sample Inside Pages, see more at **Outreach.com**

Other Booklets Available From Outreach:

On the Third Day—the miraculous story of Jesus' resurrection

God So Loved—the message of God's love and plan for salvation

The God Questions: Truth—answers to key questions about God and the Bible

The God Questions: Religions—answers the question: Do all roads (and all religions) lead to heaven?

Look for all these Outreach Booklets at your local Christian bookstore or visit **Outreach.com** for bulk quantities.

The Love Dare

The Love Dare 40-day devotional as featured in the movie FIREPROOF

As the marriage between firefighter Caleb Holt and his wife crumbles, Caleb's father sends him a book with a challenge: *The Love Dare*. Take a 40-day journey to love first, to love better and to love for a lifetime! *The Love Dare* includes a Bible-based devotional, a notes section and a love "Dare" for each of the 40 days.

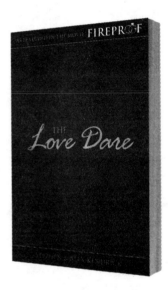

USE *THE LOVE DARE* TO BUILD AND STRENGTHEN YOUR MARRIAGE

GREAT AS A WEDDING OR ANNIVERSARY GIFT

USE AS A FOLLOW-UP OR SUPPLEMENTAL DEVOTIONAL FOR A *FIREPROOF YOUR MARRIAGE* SMALL GROUP OR CLASS

Look for *The Love Dare* at your local Christian bookstore or visit **Outreach.com** for bulk quantities.

Sample Inside Pages, see more at **Outreach.com**

Additional *Fireproof* Resources Available From **OUTREACH**